WUNT DRUV!

A SALUTE TO THE SUSSEX DIALECT

DAVID ARSCOTT

WITH ILLUSTRATIONS BY
RICHARD SCOLLINS

COUNTRYSIDE BOOKS
NEWBURY BERKSHIRE

First published 2006
© David Arscott 2006

COUNTRYSIDE BOOKS
3 Catherine Road
Newbury, Berkshire

To view our complete range of books,
please visit us at
www.countrysidebooks.co.uk

ISBN 1 84674 006 1
EAN 978 1 84674 006 0

Designed by Peter Davies, Nautilus Design
Produced through MRM Associates Ltd., Reading
Typeset by CJWT Solutions, Newton-le-Willows
Printed by Woolnough Bookbinding Ltd., Irthlingborough

CONTENTS

ACKNOWLEDGEMENTS

I am accustomed to the generosity of strangers when researching my books, but the interest shown and the help offered with this book have been exceptional. Many names appear in these pages, and I trust that their owners will feel thereby thanked, but I am also indebted to the following, whether for material lent, words and phrases supplied, contacts suggested or interviews given: Alex Askaroff, Rose and Arthur Bashford, Alice Bessant, John Branston, Helena Carter, Jack Charman, David Clark, Dennis Collins, Miles Costello, Diana Crook, Peter Davies, June Eade, Dawn Eede, Geoff Ellsworth, Jim Farrer, Glenis Fedak, Bob Fry, W. Garraway, Shirley Glaysher, Peter Gooday, Liz Gregory, John Hart, Mrs Hitchen, Shirley Kennard, Peter Kirby, Wendy Lloyd, Joan Lockwood, Bob Luckhurst, Jerry Marchant, Marion May, Roy and Vera May, Gordon Moore, Roger Newman, Ivor Noel, Mak Norman, Annie Onslow, Maurice Packham, Betty Park, John Rhodes, Veronica Ross, Melvin Smith, Pete Staniforth, Mike Tubbs, C. R. Upton, Tony Wales, Jenifer Waters, Marrion Wells, Nick Whistler, Ralfe Whistler and David Woodard.

FOREWORD

When, some years ago, I began compiling an anthology of Sussex writing, I was surprised to discover how recently it was that writers treated the county almost as foreign territory. As late as the 1930s it was still possible to describe a journey through the Downs and Weald as one might a hike through the Andes, coming upon small towns and villages the average reader had never visited and was expected to know very little about. It was common, too, to write about the Sussex character, as if a different kind of person was to be encountered – a stubborn one, typically, who *wunt be druv* – as soon as you crossed the border from Kent, Surrey or Hampshire.

I began with the not unreasonable assumption that the Sussex dialect was a long-dead language. When William Parish published his influential work on the subject in 1875, he began by regretting that 'the march of education must sooner or later trample down and stamp out anything like distinctive provincial dialect in England'. He was right: certainly, it is impossible to find any corner of the county in which people still address each other in the old way.

And yet, as soon as I began my researches, it became clear to me that those pre-war days in which travel writers 'discovered' rural Sussex must still have had their pockets of local speech, however thinned out by the steady encroachments of the outside world. The major assaults upon those last bastions of dialect were still to come – the upheavals of the war itself; the massive influx of outsiders into a rash of newly built homes once it was over; the universal language of radio and, later, television.

How much of this remnant of dialect could I yet trace? Fortunately we live longer than our forebears, and 70-year-olds are commonplace today. Many people born in Sussex around 1935 have memories of hearing traditional speech, and quite a few still have a trace of the accent, especially when remembering the old days. The parents of some spoke a more-or-less standard English, stippled with words, phrases and expressions which their own mothers and fathers had used as part of a rather more thoroughgoing Sussex, grammar and all.

Here, then, is a celebration of the Sussex tongue, some of it still spoken within living memory. Our own grandchildren will surely never hear the like.

David Arscott

CHAPTER 1

An Introduction to the Sussex Dialect

The trouble started some 500 years ago. You can conveniently blame it on William Caxton, who set up his printing press in Westminster during the 1470s (and who described his own Kentish tongue as 'brode and rude'), but the drive to create a standardized English, untainted by confusing and barbaric local variations, was irrepressible once the literate classes came out of the Latin closet and began to write predominantly in their own tongue. 'No-one who was anyone in England,' the Sussex dialect authority Richard Coates has observed, 'wrote in non-standard English after 1500, and the pressure was growing on users of non-courtly accents to abandon them.'

In view of this powerful pressure to conform, it's remarkable to find that traces of the old Sussex dialect have survived over the intervening centuries and that we can still hear the accent and some of the vocabulary on a few elderly tongues to this day.

The heyday of 'dialect retrieval' was the 19th century, by which time it was almost too late. The coming of the railways brought social mobility, and 'furriners' – predominantly Londoners – poured into Brighton and the other coastal towns, bringing their speech with them. These influences gradually spread out into the Weald, until only the remotest areas were untouched by them. Very few native speakers unselfconsciously wrote as they spoke, and the educated folk who were anxious to record the dialect for posterity necessarily had to pick up such snatches of it as they could from friendly, though not always reliable, sources.

The Victorian writer E.V. Lucas posed the question whether Sussex actually had a dialect of its own at all, since the speech of those who lived in the west chimed closely with neighbouring Hampshire, while natives of the easterly parts had linguistic affinities with Kent. This is true, however, of all county dialects in times when people travelled very little and when their speech patterns were therefore often narrowly localized. Gaius Carley, the village blacksmith at Adversane, south of Billingshurst in the early years of the 20th century, and the

7

author of a colourful memoir in colloquial English, thought that the villagers of Kirdford 'talked funny'. Adversane and Kirdford are less than seven miles apart as the crow flies.

The seminal work on the subject, to which all subsequent studies owe a greater or lesser debt, is *A Dictionary of the Sussex Dialect* by the Rev. W.D. Parish. The son of the wonderfully named diplomat and naturalist Sir Woodbine Parish, he was vicar of Selmeston, east of Lewes. His dictionary, published in 1875, is leavened with humour. Confessing that pronunciation is an almost impossible thing to pin down, he nevertheless claims to have recognized one watertight rule: 'The letter *h* is never by any chance used in its right place, and any one who has ever attempted to teach a Sussex child to read, must be convinced that nothing short of a surgical operation would ever introduce a correct pronunciation of the aspirate into his system.'

Parish went one better than Lucas, appending an *e, w* or *m* to many of his words to indicate that they were used specifically in the far east of the county (imagining a line north from Hastings), the west (north from Shoreham) or mid-Sussex (between the two). When I worked as a BBC radio producer and presenter in Sussex from the late 1970s I was able to put this to the test on Bert Winborne, a gardener of the old school, who was born in Haywards Heath in 1905 and for whom several old dialect words were commonplace. We made many programmes together before his death at the age of 97, and I grew accustomed to looking up 'new' words in Parish. Sure enough, they would almost invariably have the letter *m* beside them. Bert would, for example, talk about someone *spanneling* about – making messy footprints in the way of a muddy dog. A fallow field was a *voller*, which you might dig until you had a deep tilth, and then the ground would be 'in good heart'. A carrot that had forked, making a set of useless extra roots, was *spronky*. *Brencheese* (bread and cheese) was what an old gardener would have for lunch with his cold tea. We used a *swaphook* to hack at the weeds on the allotment we developed together. Covering plants with soil on a temporary basis, we would 'heal them up'. And I was urged to *look peert*, which is to say lively, when I set about a job.

Other words Bert used weren't regionalized by Parish: the prongs on our forks were *speens*, and the stalks of fruit were *strigs*. When there was rain in the air it was *shucky* weather, while if you wanted to transport water around the garden in a container on wheels you used a *bodge*. At least once the Sussex pronunciation completely fooled me: in *The Upstart Gardener*, the account I wrote of Bert's life and our vegetable growing together, I had him talking about the 'arms' of the broad beans, the dead stalks ready for the compost. What he was actually referring to (as one kind reader pointed out to me) were the 'haulms'.

Nick Turner, born during the last war, recalls the speech of his family, who were woodmen in mid Sussex. Not only did they use words that Parish missed, he says, but they had a way of pronouncing basic English which was barely intelligible to an outsider. *Welmsay*, for instance, was 'Well, I mean to say', while *ferdigit* was 'for to get'.

'My grandfather was a bit of a local character, but my regular fishing pal had never met him. One day I had go up to see him for my father and invited my mate to come along. I did what I had to do and chatted for 15 minutes or so before leaving. Once back in the car I asked my mate what he thought of the old chap, and his reply was: "Well, he seemed nice enough, but I didn't understand a word either of you said."'

As it happens we have an excellent guide to mid-Sussex pronunciation at an earlier period in the journal (1785–90) and correspondence of John Burgess. Born in Ditchling, he later emigrated to America, and his letters home are a rare example of completely natural, unaffected writing in the dialect. Burgess clearly pronounced 'kettle' as *kittle*, 'week' as *wick*, 'spoil' as *spile*, 'since' as *sence* and 'believed' as *beleft*, because that's just how he wrote the words down.

Parish attempts to codify speech habits such as this. Here are some of his findings:

- *a* before *ll* is made to sound like *o*, 'tallow' becoming *toller* and 'fallow' becoming *foller* (which takes us back to Bert's summer *voller*)
- *a* before *t* is expanded into *ea*, so that 'gate' stretches across two syllables as *ge'at* and 'mate' is heard as *me'at*
- *o* before *n* is expanded into *oa*, 'don't' becoming *do'ant*
- *o* before *r* is pronounced *ah*: 'corn' is *carn* and 'morning' is *marning*
- *ee* becomes *i* in words such as 'week' and 'sheep': across Sussex 'sheep' are the *ship* which shouldn't be spoiled (or *spiled*) for a ha'p'orth of tar which would heal their cuts at shearing time.
- *i*, on the other hand, becomes *ee*, with *meece* for 'mice'
- elsewhere *i* becomes *e*, with *pet* for 'pit' and *spet* for 'spit'
- *e* can become an open *a*: *rackon* for 'reckon'.

As for consonants, *double t* is pronounced as *d* ('little' becomes *liddle*). A final -*st* is given an extra vowel in the plural, a habit which teachers tried to drum out of their little charges by reciting this rhyme:

I saw three ghosteses sitting on posteses,
Eating hot toasteses.
The butter ran down their fisteses,
Dirty little beasteses.

Another feature of the old dialect was the transposition of letters or sounds in some words:

clapse = clasp
gurt = great
perramble = preamble
purty = pretty
split = spoilt
wapses = wasps

In the far east of Sussex, just to confuse matters a little further, *th* was sounded as *d*, with *dat* for 'that', *dem* for 'them', and so on.

To get the feel of the old spoken Sussex, here are some common words followed by their dialect equivalents – not very different, but pretty confusing to an incomer when strung together in a rambling sentence.

absit = absent
acrost = across
aig = egg
arder = adder
afeared = afraid
arter = after
agin = against
amost = almost
allus = always
ax = ask
barr'r = barrow
b'luv = believe
bline = blind
bile = boil
'card'nly = accordingly
clim = climb
clitch = clutch
crownation = coronation

crass = cross
dasent = decent
draat = draught
drillaty = dilatory
druv = driven
durmut = turnip
dursn't = dare not
erne = heron
fambly = family
farder, farver = father
frit = frightened
fust = first
girt, gurt = great
git = get
go'ast = ghost
grinstone = grindstone
holp = helped
jes = just

ketch = catch
mars, mas, mass = master
maun = must not
mek = make
mesh = marsh
mistus = mistress
mout = might
mun = must
mus = mister
muvver = mother
nary = not any
naythur = neither
naun = nothing
'ood = wood
'ooman = woman
ornary = ordinary
pharisees = fairies
pint = point
prapper = propper
prensley = presently
rip = reap
robbut = rabbit
rubbish = rubbidge

sartin = certain
scritch = screech
sen = since
sin = seen
sodger = soldier
spadger = sparrow
spartacles = spectacles
'speck = expect
spile = spoil
squrrl = squirrel
strick = strict
soor = swore
tek = take
tarble = terrible
turmut = turnip
varmint, varmunt = vermin
wo'ak = oak
wunt = won't
worrited = worried
wrastle = wrestle
wuts = oats
yarb = herb
'zackly = exactly

A true dialect has a distinctive grammatical structure as well as the more obvious differences of pronunciation and vocabulary. Native speakers would have used *yourn, hern* and *theirn* for possessives, and 'himself' would commonly be *hisself*. In the past tense 'he came' would be *he come*, with *they was* for 'they were' and *she give* for 'she gave'. But there were local differences here, too. In the west of the county you would say *I en't done it* and *she ben't here*, whereas in the east the usage was *ain't* and *bain't*.

What follows in this book must therefore be regarded as approximate, the words, expressions, conversations caught (or invented) at a particular time and relating to a particular place. There was a Sussex dialect, but it was a shifting, kaleidoscopic thing, liable to *git an uppish sheere-man mortacious vlothered, I bluv*!

Humpty Dumpty

CHAPTER 2

A Look at
Sussex Place-Names

T he first village I lived in when I came to Sussex was Albourne ('alder stream'), near Hurstpierpoint. My neighbours – all from outside – called it Al-bourne with an open a, but I noted that the BBC pronunciation dictionary preferred Awl-bourne, as did quite a few other local people. In order to settle the matter once and for all, I went to see an elderly woman in The Street whose family had lived and farmed in the area for many years. Miss Fanny Hole was in no doubt at all: 'It's Ahl-bourne', she said.

The shifting sands of pronunciation are nothing to the whirlpools of derivation. While even the experts argue about the finer points of it (a close knowledge of various languages and their dialects is essential), amateur romantics and fantasists are unable to resist spinning engaging yarns to 'explain' a name. So Blackboys, near Heathfield, must refer to the iron industry which once flourished in the weald: as the men emerged filthy from their charcoal-burning, their neighbours would refer in suitably graphic terms to the spot in which they lived and worked. Common sense immediately asks some questions. The iron industry has, indeed, given its name to features such as woods, fields and roads (Furnace Green, and so on), but why would this one workplace deserve to be singled out among so many? Were those neighbours themselves not engaged in the industry in any case? And why should the inhabitants not choose their own, less derogatory, name for their hamlet? But the best way of refuting such derivations is through research: ah, it transpires that there was a Richard Blakeboy in the area in 1398. Enough said.

The majority of our town and village names are Anglo-Saxon in origin. True, Celtic people were here first, and the Romans were in charge for some four hundred years, but the Germanic takeover and makeover from around AD 450 was incredibly thorough. Danish invaders certainly gave the language some core vocabulary, but Sussex became the kingdom of the South Saxons, as the name implies, and the great King Alfred ensured that the Viking horde was kept at bay, so forestalling any further significant outside influence on the local language until the Normans arrived in 1066. Dozens of Sussex places are named after

Charcoal burners, photographed in Balcombe Forest in the early 20th century

people, many of them having the -ingas suffix (denoting 'people of'): someone called Angemaer was an influential figure in what was to become Angmering, while Flecci was the boss man in Fletching. Not all -*ing* endings or component parts refer to people, however. Similarly confusion often arises between *hām*, meaning 'settlement' (as in Patcham), and *hamm*, which refers to land enclosed by water, marsh or higher ground (Udiam).

Here are some more common place-name elements, with an example of each:

æsc	ash tree	Ashdown
bēce, bōc	beech tree	Cowbeech
beorg, berg	mound, barrow	Hunter's Burgh
brōc	brook, stream	Blackbrook
brycg	bridge	Elbridge
burh (dative byrig)	stronghold	Cissbury
burna	stream	Aldingbourne
ceaster	Roman town	Chichester
cumb	short, round-ended valley	Balcombe
denn	woodland pasture	Denne Park
denu	long-steep-sided valley	Balsdean
dūn	hill, down	Ecclesden

ēg	island, area of higher ground	Thorney
feld	open land	Uckfield
ford	ford	Ford
hæth	heather, heathland	Heathfield
holt	wood	Wiggonholt
hyll	hill	Broomhill
hyrst	wooded hill	Warminghurst
lēah	(woodland) clearing	Ardingly
lind	lime tree, linden	Lindfield
mere	pool	Falmer
mersc	marsh	Peasmarsh
stede	place, site	Buxted
stig	path	Ansty(e)
stræt	Roman road	Streat
tēah	close, enclosure, tye	Brambletye
tūn	farmstead, village	Alciston
wīc	specialized farm, processing or manufacturing place	Aldwick
wudu	wood	Manhood

These names are from the language of our forebears some 1,500 years ago, but the traces of dialect words from a slightly later period can also be found in our place-names. Coneyhurst, for example, reminds us that the American word for 'rabbits' was once our own. The fact that the animals weren't introduced to England until the 12th century (when they soon became a valued source of meat), tells us that this settlement must have been medieval. Jugg's Road in Lewes was formerly known as Juggs Borstal: *jugs* were Brighton fishermen, and this was the steep downland track (or *bostal*) their wives followed to sell their catch in the county town.

After the Conquest, French words began to colour the language, and they've left their mark on place-names. Beachy Head was *Beauchef* (*beau* + *chef* 'beautiful headland'), so that its modern name contrives to give it two heads. Bewbush, in Crawley, was *Beau Buis* or beautiful thicket, while Bells Yew Green, on the Kent border, has nothing to do with trees or bells, being *Bels Leius*, or 'beautiful place'. Battle, of course, was *La Batailge*, where the Battle of Hastings took place. Caldbec Hill, where much of the fighting took place, is pure Scandinavian for 'cold stream' but likewise came with the Normans.

Ownership of much of the land passed to the victorious invaders, some of whom imprinted their names on the places they held. Hurstpierpoint and

Sheep drinking from a dew pond at Falmer, on the Sussex Downs

Herstmonceux bear the stamp respectively of the de Pierpoint and Monceaux families.

Although most names were established long ago, Brighton is an example of a spelling that has changed to match the pronunciation. Orginally it was *Beorhthelmes tun*, 'farmstead of the leader known as Beorhthelm' (whose name was composed of elements meaning 'bright' and 'helmet'). Even into the 19th century it was commonly spelt as *Brighthelmstone* or something similar (standardized spelling, we must remember, is a relatively recent thing), but by then it had long been shortened to Brighton on the tongue. The more common practice in modern times is for the spelling to dictate the sound, especially as so many of today's inhabitants have arrived in Sussex from outside. When I worked for the BBC here we were concerned to get our pronunciations right (I still recall my amused horror when I heard a colleague refer on air to Slaugham as *slorm*, when he should have said *slaffam*, while another gave us *larf-tn* for Laughton), but this wasn't always an easy business. The 'lyes' were straightforward enough, with a stress on the final syllable of places such as Ardingly, Chiddingly, Hellingly and West Hoathly (arding-*ly*, etc.), although East Hoathly, we were assured, was hoath-*lee*. And Seaford we treated in traditional fashion as a spondee, in other words, giving equal weight to each of its syllables, although we were aware that the incomers had almost succeeded in refashioning their town as *sea*-fud.

But what should we do with Burwash? An old rhyme goes 'To love and to cherish/from Battle to Berrish'. What dialect speakers did with the e is open to debate: perhaps the sounds were closer to *churrish* and *burrish*, and that's a pronunciation that survives at least in folk memory. We decided, I think rightly, that this should now be regarded as an archaism – a battle that had been lost. Certainly a reincarnated Sussex countryman of yesteryear would have great trouble finding the place today merely by asking directions (few would understand him), but he would be pretty perplexed about quite a few other things, too: not progress, but change.

Arthur Beckett, founder-editor of the old *Sussex County Magazine*, told the story of a visitor from outside the county who was looking for a Mr Pocock of Alciston. The labourer he asked professed not to have a clue about either the person or the place, until someone usefully pointed out that he was the very man himself. 'Why,' was his pugnacious response, 'you should ha' axed fur Mus Palk of Ahson!'

Some local pronunciations:

Alciston	Ahson	Firle	Furrel
Arundel	Arndel	Hailsham	Helsum
Bodiam	Bodg'm	Heathfield	Heffel
Bosham	Bozz'm	Pevensey	Pemsey
Chalvington	Chawton	Sedlescombe	Sailsc'm
Chichester	Chiddester	Selmeston	Simson
Easebourne	Ezb'n	Udiam	Udg'm
Etchingham	Ech'm		

There are, of course, plenty of curiosities to be found on a map of Sussex, some of them marking a particular historical moment, some demonstrating misplaced human ingenuity, and others resistant to a conclusive interpretation. Muster Green is among the first batch. Sussex didn't see a great deal of action during the English Civil War, but the first major skirmish was at Haywards Heath in 1642, and it was at this spot that the troops gathered. (For the record, the Royalists were soundly beaten.) Newhaven, similarly, can be precisely dated. The River Ouse once wound down from Lewes to the sea at medieval Seaford, but the port became silted up and unusable: an artificial cut was made in 1539 to a spot near the coastal village of Meeching, which became the 'new haven'. Telegraph Hill in the west of the county was, indeed, the site of a signalling station – one of several which transmitted semaphore messages between Portsmouth dockyard and the Admiralty in London during the Napoleonic wars.

Chiddingly Village, Sussex.

Cade Street, recalling the rebel Jack Cade, seems also to fit into the first category, but it may well be a candidate for the second, the made-up variety. This hamlet was known as Cat Street as late as the mid-17th century – in other words, two hundred years after the 1450 uprising. A large roadside memorial claims that this is the spot at which Cade was killed, a fact which is itself open to question. The suspicion must be that a conveniently similar name was changed to suit a colourful story.

You might expect rivers to have borne their names from antiquity, but this is not always so. The one that runs down to Shoreham was formerly known as Bramber Water, and it was given the name Adur as recently as 1612 by Michael Drayton in his topographical work *Polyolbion*. This was simply a mistake. Drayton believed that the Roman Portus Adurni, which is now thought to be Portsmouth, lay at the mouth of the river and so named it accordingly.

Just along from Shoreham is what the Ordnance Survey map says is Kingston by Sea. Recorded as *Chingestune* in Domesday, meaning 'royal manor', it was later named after the de Busci family. The 'by Sea' suffix occurs as early as 1730, and it is, indeed, by the sea, but Kingston Buci was how the locals knew it, until very recent times at least.

As for our third category, the head-scratchers, Pease Pottage (south of Crawley) is perhaps exhibit number one. Back in 1724 it was Peasepottage Gate, on the edge of Peasepottage Forest. It's said that prisoners on their way to Horsham Gaol would rest at this spot and be given a dish of cold pottage, a mash of boiled peas. Not entirely convincing, perhaps, but can you think of a better explanation?

CHAPTER 3

A Selection of Personal Names

Passing on a surname to your offspring wasn't the norm among ordinary folk until about the 14th century, by which time the Black Death must have wiped out quite a few of them, but once a name had managed to become established it tended to flourish within a particular area. Dialect was narrowly localized precisely because people moved around very little, marrying people close to hand.

The folk singer Shirley Collins remembers talking to Fanny Eastwood at Etchingham in the 1970s.

'She and her husband Will were in their eighties then, and both were Sussex born and bred. I asked her if she'd ever had any other sweetheart but him. "I did," she said. "And why didn't you marry him?" "Oh," she replied, "he was too outlandish." It turned out that she meant he came from a village two miles away!'

Bob Lomas, brought up in the Storrington area, recalls the consternation caused by the arrival of some 'furriners' in a local village when he was a small boy. Since he was born in 1934, this can't have been much before the last war.

'My mother was talking to some local women when the bus came in and a family got off. They came from the next village, which was two-and-a-half miles away. And the talking stopped until one of the women said, "What are they doing over here, then?" And that was in my lifetime.'

Ray Chris, the same age as Bob, remembers that families stayed in the same village for generations, and that sometimes a name would be widespread there.

'When I lived over at Lurgashall they used to say that if you passed someone at night in the dark you'd say "Good night, Mr Singleton", and you'd nearly always be right.'

'Mind you,' he adds, 'in the Horsham area there were families called Hogflesh and Sweetapple, and they seem to have completely died out.'

Bob Lewis, born in 1936, similarly recalls the clustering of names in the Midhurst area, where he was brought up.

'You could virtually identify the village someone came from. If he said he was a Tupper you knew he came from Heyshott. About 70 per cent of the village was

Tuppers. The classic thing was you looked on the village noticeboard for the cricket fixture, and the cricket team would be A. Tupper, B. Tupper, C. Tupper, and so on, sometimes with a nickname. You could reckon that 50 or 60 per cent of them would have the one family name.

'If you went to Cocking it would be the Knights. I worked with Boy Knight, and there was a whole lot of them in Cocking. If you went to Graffham it was all Challens. They were all related to one another at that time of day.'

How many Tuppers are there in Heyshott today?

The thinning out of the dialect thus went hand-in-hand with the dispersal of family names. Here are some traditional Sussex names still to be found in the phone book, even if their owners have strayed some way from home:

Blann	Noakes
Charman	Packham
Coppard	Penfold
Cruttenden	Scrase
Dudeney	Stenning
Dudman	Tester
Elphick	Tuppen
Fuller	Tupper
Gearing/Geering	Venner
Izard/Izzard	Verrall
Mepham	Voller

Another name to persist in the Brighton area (it was once common in the fishing community) is Mighall, pronounced **my**-all. The story goes that it derives from Spanish *Miguel*, and that the earliest local bearers of the name were sailors left behind after the destruction of the Armada in 1588. In truth, it probably comes from the popular, rather than learned, French form of Michael.

Christian names are, by contrast, subject to fashion, and there has never been a worse time for a sensitive child to be born to a non-conformist family than the period from the late 16th century. Puritans saddled their youngsters with names intended to remind them of their Christian duty, my favourite being Fly Fornication Richardson of Waldron. Our dialect glossary reveals that 'fornication' was commonly used to mean idleness, so that the growing lad may not have been perpetually dogged by a struggle against sexual licence, but that was surely of little consolation to him.

Was one of these Hastings' fishermen called Mighall, I wonder?

All of these names were shamelessly given to Sussex children:

Accepted	No-merit
Churchyard	Obydyence
Comfort	Preserved
Craven	Redeemed
Dedicate	Refraine
Elected	Rejoyce
Fight-the-good-fight-of-faith	Renewed
Freegift	Repent
Goodgifte	Silence
Kill-sin	Sin–Deny
Lament	Soryforsine
Laud-on-high	Stand-fast-on-high
Learnwysdom	Temperance
Mercy	Thankful
More-fruit	The-Peace-of-God
Muchmarcy	Weep-not
Muchmorefruite	

At Warbleton in the summer of 1588, just after the Spanish Armada had been defeated, two baby boys were christened Bethankfull Durrant and Preserved Holman. It could have been worse for them. Years later, in the same parish, two families conjured names for their children which, while not Puritan, were real horrors: Onnion Leafe and Obadiah Orange Lemon.

CHAPTER 4

Meet the Cladpoles

As dialect was seen to be waning, several writers made a valiant attempt to capture its essence. One of the earliest was Richard Lower (1782–1865), who was born at Alfriston and became the village schoolmaster at Muddles Green near Chiddingly. 'Dickie' Lower, as he was known, regularly turned local events into verse for the *Sussex Advertiser*, and he wrote two doggerel poems in the dialect under the name Tim Cladpole. (Inevitably, perhaps, there was an emphasis on the humorous, and some of his 'rustic' readers were none too happy about being portrayed as simpletons.) The first was entitled 'Tom Cladpole's Jurney to Lunnun' and the second 'Jan Cladpole's Trip to 'Merricur'. Here's a snatch of the former. (His 'haboot' is a half-boot, and the 'aluss' is an alehouse.)

> Now whislin up de grove I goos,
> Close by ol' Grinder's Mill.
> Birds sung an seem'd to cheer me up
> As I went down de hill.
>
> Many long miles I shuffled on,
> As fast as I could goo;
> At last I gun to feel, ya see,
> De haboot ring ma toe.
>
> A liddle aluss stood close by –
> Thinks I, I'll go in here
> And git, ya see, a coger loike,
> Ov good brencheese an' beer
>
> De ooman ge a bit o' rag
> About ma toe to tye,
> I thank'd ur for't, mopp'd up de beer
> An off agin went I!

Now wost ant was, I couldn't read
   De letters on de post,
So sumtimes I went roun about
   An otherwile was lost!

I howsumever trudg'd away,
   An see de sun went down,
Jest as I cum upon de brow
   Dat leads to Crayton town.

So now, think I, I think I'll stay
   An ax um fer a lodgin;
An when de mornen cums agen,
   Why den I can be bodgin.

De aluss stood upon de right
   And was both big an fine,
An had I think (but 'most furgit)
   A Jack Ass for a sine!

I see'd a man upon the step –
   'Well, measter,' den I sed,
'If I stop here wot wol ye charge
   A fellur fer a bed?'

At first he bawled out rather bruss,
   And den he squirr'd aroun,
Much loike a pegtap, den said he,
   'Why on'ny half-a-crown.'

'What! half-a-crown for one poor snore?'
   Good lack how I did stare!
'Den get along ya clown,' sed he,
   And den he gun to swear.

If 'twant fer gitten in a scrape
   About dis half-a-crown,
I'd us'd ma ashen swish abit
   And lay'd de dandy down.

23

Nursery Rhymes

The Grand Old Duke of York

CHAPTER 5

A Sussex Dictionary

As has already been noted, the Sussex dialect did not fit neatly inside the county boundaries: some of the words listed below would have been found further afield, while others were used within a relatively narrow sphere. A few, indeed, will have been one-offs, heard by a 'collector' who found them irresistible.

a-bed	in bed
abouten	about to, but always used in the past tense: '*I was abouten going out, when ...*'
abroad	in all directions; all about
abuseful/abusefully	
	abusive; in an abusive manner
account	reputation, esteem
ache	to tire
ackle	to manage something: '*I can't ackle it.*'
addle/ardle	ill; diseased; slightly unwell – **adle-headed** stupid
adin	within
adone	to leave off
adry	thirsty
aggy	peevish; out of sorts
all one	all the same
allow	to give as an opinion; to conclude
alltsinit	merely
along-of	on account of
amakin	wild: '*She drives me amakin.*'
ampery	weak, unhealthy
an/on	of: '*She wants to be rid an him.*'

anywhen/anywhiles
at any time

argify
signify; import: '*It do'ant argify much whether i goos today or whether i goos tomorrow*'.

arney
in a bad temper

arse backards
back to front

aside
bankrupt: 'William Walder went aside this evening'.

aslew
slanting

atween
between

atwixt
betwixt, between

axey
the ague

babbins
wood for fire-lighting

backturned
turned away from: '*He was backturned when I saw him*'. = 'He was standing with his back to me'.

backwent
going away: '*I only saw him backwent*' = 'I only saw him as he was going away from me'

badskin
ill-tempered

badwekyn
a blue and white hanging for a bed

ballies
belly

balsam
uncomplimentary backchat

bannick
to beat; a severe beating

barca
tobacco

bark
to cough

barton
the demesne of a manor; the manor house itself, or its outhouses and yards

bat
(1) a stick of any kind (2) *usually plural* a log of wood for burning, or any odd piece of wood

bat and trap
a game played chiefly on Good Friday

bavins
(pronounced *bah-vn*) brushwood, faggots

bawl
to read aloud

Playing bat and trap in Brighton c.1930s (Ralph Merrifield)

be at	to attend to: '*The doctor's been at 'er for a week.*'
beat the devil round the gooseberry bush	
	to tell a long rigmarole
beazled	exhausted, tired out
beever	eleven o'clock luncheon
behither	on this side, rather than beyond
behopes	'let us hope'
be how tel/be 'ow dil	
	shortened form of *let be how 'twill* = 'let the consequences be what they may'
beleft	past tense of to believe: '*I never should have beleft it.*'
belikes	very likely
bellick	to bellow
bethanks	thank goodness
bettermost	superior, often used with 'rather', e.g. '*rather bettermost sort of folks*'
bibber	to shake and rattle, as a window
bidance	abode
birds' wedding day	St Valentine's Day
bitten/bitenous	inclined to bite
bittle-battle	the game of stoolball

Playing bittle-battle in Horsham Park, 1878

black-eyed Susan	pond pudding; a well pudding with plums or raisins in it
blackthorn winter	a cold spell in early spring when the blackthorn blossom is out
blanket pudding	a long pudding made with flour and jam. Also called **bolster pudding**.
bleat	(of the wind) cold; cutting
blobitt/blob tongue	a telltale
blue-go	an out-of-the-way occurrence: '*Ah, that war a blue-go, warn't ut.*'
blunder	the sound as of something heavy falling
bly	a resemblance; a general likeness
bobbing needle	a bodkin
bob	a beetle
bodge	a cask on wheels
boffled	browbeaten
borns	the days of one's life, as in '*all my borns*'
bottley	a glass marble from the neck of a bottle
bough-house	a private house allowed to be open at fairs for the sale of liquor
brabagious	(an ill-defined *adjective*, possibly meaning something akin to 'vexatious', as in '*you nasty brabagious creature*')
brack	a mark: '*It's as good as new, without a brack on it.*'
brandirons	firedogs; iron supports for burning logs in a fireplace
brave/bravely	in good health; prosperous: '*I'm bravely, thank you.*'
bread and cheese friend	a true friend
brenbutter	a slice of buttered bread
brencheese	bread and cheese
brish	as quickly as possible
broad	(of a place) smaller than another with which it is compared: '*Walsted is a little broad of Lindfield*'

bruss	someone who speaks bluntly and briskly
bumblesome	hunched up; misfitting; clumsy
burnish	to grow fat
by then	by the time that: *'By then you've come back I'll have done it.'*
cackleberrry	an egg
caddling	the act of looking around for odd jobs
cadey	a hat
call	reason: *'You ain't got no call to worry.'*
call over	to abuse
callow	smooth, bare
catch hot	to get a fever
catch hurt	to meet with an accident
Catlick	Roman Catholic
catterning	the custom of begging for apples and beer on St Catherine's Day
certain sure	most certainly
chance-born	an illegitimate child. Also called **come-by-chance**
change	a shirt; a shift
chank	to chew
chapel master	a Nonconformist preacher
charm stuff	ague medicine
chat	a very small potato
chavee	a young child
chizzly	gritty; harsh and dry to the teeth;
chockly	dry
chog	choked up, eg a garden chog with weeds
chuckle-headed	stupid
chuff	churlish, surly
church litten	a churchyard

A Sussex Look at

Nursery Rhymes

Little Jack Horner

churchyarder	a bad cough
clam	a cold sweat
clapper	the tongue
clawney	ancestors; relations
cleat	a wooden wedge used to prevent a door or gate from swinging
clemmening	the custom of going from house to house asking for apples and beer on St Clement's Day, the blacksmiths' festival
clip	to hold on to
cluck	out of spirits
clumpety foot	club root, a disease of brassicas
clutch	close; tightly
clutter up	to throw into confusion; to crowd
coarse	harsh, rough-tongued
cocker up	to spoil; to gloss over with an air of truth; to invent a story
codger	a miser
cog	to entice
coger	a meal of bread, cheese and beer
commence	a job; an affair: 'Here's a pretty commence.'
common	quite well in health (compare brave); genuine; without false airs and graces
concerned in liquor	
	drunk
contrairy	disagreeble; obstinately self-willed
contraption	contrivance; management
coolthe	coolness
coombe/combe	a downland hollow
countable	accountable
cousins, to call	to be on intimate terms, but generally used negatively: 'She and I do'ant call cousins at all.'
crank/cranky	merry; cheerful; drunk
crazy	out of order; dilapidated
cuckoo gate	a kissing gate

WUNT BE DRUV!

curious	unsteady; drunk
cuss	surly; shrewish
Cut your stick!	Be off!
dang/dannel	exclamation expressing anger, surprise or frustration, substituted for damn
dappen	by the time that: 'Dappen I've done this job I'll come and lend yer a hand.'
darling/dawlin	the smallest pig of a litter; runt; an unhealthy child
dead alive	dull; heavy, stupid
deedy	clever; industrious
denial	a hindrance: '*His deafness is a great denial to him.*'
dereaway	thereabouts
devourous	voracious
dinlow	slow-witted
dish of tongues	a scolding
disremember	to forget
doddle	to wag; to tremble; to walk infirmly
done over	tired out
dosset/dozzle	a small portion
down	laid up by illness
down bed	a bed on the floor
dracly minute	immediately
raggle tail	a slut
dree	unpleasant, as of weather or a place
rugged	(of linen etc.) half dried
drythe	drought; thirst
duffer	a peddlar
dunch	deaf; slow to comprehend
dunnamy	don't know how many
dunnamuch	don't know how much
dunnick	a privy over an open cesspit

dusty	off colour; '*I'm not too dusty, thank you*', meaning that one isn't too bad
Dutch cousins	great friends
duzzick/dezzick	a hard day's work
eddel	rotten
e'enamost	nearly
elynge	solitary, isolated; uncanny, eerie
end on	in a great hurry
ernful	sad; lamentable
eye and limb	to curse: '*He eyed and limbed me*.'
faddy	fanciful
faggot	a good-for-nothing girl
fail	to fall ill
fan	to banter; to tease
favour	to resemble; resemblance
fegs!	(an exclamation)
fid	to work too hard at anything
fight	to flog
file	a cunning, deceitful person
fill-dick	the month of February, when ditches become full of rainwater
fire spannel	a lazy person
flarksy	smart; showy, ostentatious
flasket	a clothes basket; a shallow washing tub
fleed	the fat of a pig before it is melted into lard. *Fleed cakes* are made with pig's fat
flit milk	skimmed milk
floater	a suet dumpling. Also called **swimmer**
flog	to tire; to be weary
flushy	swampy

Have got as fat as a Sussex—

AND—

" wunt be druv " from Brighton.

fluttergrub	a man who delights in working in the dirt
foredoor	the front door
foreright	forthright, plain spoken; rude; obstinate
fornicate	to dawdle
foundle	anything that has been found
fourthrows/fourwents	a place where four roads meet; a crossways
Frenchy	a foreigner of any nationality who cannot speak English
fur my heel	to annoy: *'She really did fur my heel'.*
furriner	a stranger; anyone from outside Sussex
gagy	showery
gamel	to romp about
ganse	merriment, hilarity
gansing gay	cheerful; lively
gay ground	a flower garden
gifty	unwholesome; poisonous
gigglesome	given to giggling
gimsy	smartly dressed
glincy	(of ice) glassy; smooth and slippery
gobbet	a mouthful of anything
gong farmer	a cleaner-out of privies
gooder	a woman who went from house to house goodening – collecting money for Christmas – on St Thomas's day, December 21st.
goodman	an old form of address to the master of the house
grabby	grimy, filthy
grig	(1) merry, happy (2) a wag
grizzle	to fret; to grieve
grom	dirty; to soil or make dirty
grout-headed	stupidly noisy
grummut	an awkward boy
gryst	a family's weekly allowance of flour
gummut	a lout; a stupid fellow

guttermud	A simile for intimacy: 'They two be just so thick as guttermud'.
habern	the back of a grate; a fireback
haitch	a light passing shower
haitchy	misty
half-baptized	privately baptized; foolish
hap	perhaps
hard dick	Sussex pudding, which is made of flour and water only
harness	temper, mood: 'Master's in purty good harness this morning'.
hassock	anything growing in a thick matted state; a tuft of grass
head	face: 'I told him to his head.'
heggling	vexatious, trying, wearisome
helve	to gossip
hem	damn: 'I'll be hemmed if I'll be druv!'
hindertain	to delay (a blend of 'hinder' and 'detain')
hindsideafore	the wrong way round
hither	nearer: 'He's in the hither croft'.
hoak	a false excuse; pretence
honey bread	bread and honey
hopping John	soup poured on bread
horn fair	rough music made with frying pans, horns, etc., generally reserved for people whose matrimonial difficulties have attracted the attention of their neighbours
hotpot	hot ale and spirits
hover	looking cold and shivery
howler	a boy who went round wassailing the orchards, 'now nearly obsolete', wrote Parish
howsomever	however
huck	a peapod
huckle bone	the small bone found in the joint of the knee of a sheep, used by children for playing the game of dibs
huff	to scold; to take to task
hunch	a nudge

hurr	tart; rough-tasting
idle	mischievous; rude
ingenurious	ingenious
innardly	inaudibly; inwardly
innings	land enclosed from the sea
jacket	to flog
jacketting	a hard day's work
jack up	to give up on something, perhaps in anger
jackdaws' parliament	many people talking at once
jawled out	fatigued
jiggered	surprised
jobation/jawbation	a reprimand
Johnny/Lord John	the ague
jossing block	a stone mounting block, often seen at the gate of a country churchyard in Sussex – *joss up to mount* (a horse)
jostle	to cheat
journey	a day's work
jub	to move slowly and heavily, like a sluggish horse
justly	exactly
kelter/kilter	condition
kiddle	to entice, coax; to tease; to tickle
kink	to twist, entangle
knap	to shape a flint by striking it
know	knowledge: '*Poor fellow, he's got no know whatsumdever.*'
lamentable	very
lapsy	slow; lazy; stupid
late	dark. '*It gets late early these evenings.*'
lavant	an intermittent, rushing stream
lean	unprofitable
lear/leer	thin; hungry; faint
learn	to teach
leave be	to let be

lent	a loan
lew	sheltered from the wind
lewth	shelter
libbet	a short stick thrown by boys to dislodge walnuts etc. from trees
lippy	impertinent
liver	temper, mood: *'He's in a bad liver today.'*
lodge	an outhouse; a shed
long dog	the greyhound
long net	a net favoured by poachers for catching rabbits
lordings	the best kind of faggots
lourdy	heavy, sluggish
loving mud	heavy sussex clay, which clings
lurry	to hurry over work in a careless, slovenly manner
Luton	a projection from a house, such as a bow window
maid	a child of either sex who is too young to work
magnify	matter; signify: *'It do'ant magnify anyways.'*
make or mend	to interfere
maunder	to mutter or grumble; to wander about thoughtfully
mawk	a sluttish girl
mawkin	a scarecrow
maxon	a manure heap
mayhap	perhaps
mev	past tense of move: *'I mev here a year ago.'*

Tackling the loving mud on a Sussex path

mind	to remember
mislook	to misread: '*I mislooked the clock.*'
misword	a cross, angry or abusive word
mizmaze	confusion
mock-beggar hall	a house which is imposing on the outside but bare and dirty within
moil	trouble, vexation
moithered	worn out; perplexed
morning's wood	small pieces of wood for lighting a fire
mortacious/mortal	very, very much: '*I be mortal tired.*'
most-in-general	usually
mother	to take care of
muddle about	to do a little work
music	a musical instrument of any kind: '*It's a very fine music.*'
nabble	to chatter; to gossip; to idle about
napery	table linen
nary	not any
naun-but	only
near	stingy
neighbour's fare	the same bad luck as another's
nestle about	to do a little work in and out of the house
news	to tell; to disseminate: '*It was newsed about.*'
niff	to quarrel; to take offence
nip	a stingy fellow
nohows	in no way
nonce	purpose, intent, design
no-one-wheres	nowhere
no ought	no right: '*You had no ought to do it.*'
nose holes	nostrils
nottable	thrifty; industrious
noways	in no way
nubbly	lumpy; full of small clods
nunting	awkward looking

oakam	nonsense
obedience	a bow or curtsey
old father	the person who gives away the bride at her wedding
ornary	inferior; unwell
orts	odds and ends
othersome	some other, otherwise: '*Sometimes my old gal's better than what she be othersome.*'
otherwheres	at some other place
otherwhile(s)	sometimes; occasionally
over Will's mother's	in the distance; at a place some little distance away: '*It's dark over Will's mother's.*'
packled	speckled
paddle	to trample about in the wet and dirt
palm	the catkin of the pussy willow, worn on Palm Sunday
parget	to cover an external wall or part of a building with plaster or mortar, typically with decorative patterning
parly/parley Francy	to speak French or some other unintelligible language
particular	unwell: '*He's looking very particular.*'
passel	a flock; a collection of things
peaked	fretful; unwell
peert	lively
peeze	to ooze out; to leak
peg away	to eat or drink voraciously
pell	a broad shallow stretch of water, larger than an ordinary pond
perk up	to toss the head disdainfully
pest	exclamation expressing frustration or anger: '*What the pest has become of the watering pot?*'
pharisee	fairy
picksome	dainty
pillar	a large thick stack of white clouds
pithered	gummed-up

pize	(the pize) expression of surprise or annoyance in questions or exclamations: '*What the pize have you got to do with it?*'
plaguey	troublesome
pollard	the impurities left in the process of sifting flour
polt	a hard, driving blow
pooch	to push or dig into anything
poor	thin
posnet	a small saucepan or skillet
pountle	honest; reliable
powd	a boil
prayers-going	a religious service, especially in a chapel
prensley	presently; now
primed	somewhat tipsy
prodigog	Protestant
prostrate with dismal	overcome with sadness (a glorious Copper family saying)
pucker	a fuss; extreme anxiety
puckered up	shrivelled with cold
queer	to puzzle: '*It's queered me for a long time.*'
quiddy?	'What do you say?'
quilly	goose flesh
quisby	(of weather) unsettled
quotted	satiated; glutted
rabbits	exclamation of surprise, frustration, etc.
rafty	ill-tempered; difficult to manage
rash	(of a fire in frosty weather) fierce and clear
rathe	early: '*rathe in the morning*'
rattlebone	worn out; falling to pieces
recollects	memory: '*I quite lost my recollects.*'
redeem	to consider; to give an opinion
reek	fog or mist rising from the marsh

ridge bone	the weather boarding on the outside of wooden houses
rookery	a disturbance, a fuss; chattering
rough	passionate; angry
round frock	a loose outer garment worn by country people to protect their clothing
roupey	hoarse
sabbed	wet, saturated, sopping
sad	sodden; heavy; (of bread, cakes, etc.) not risen well
sare	withered, dry
sarment	sermon
sarternoon	this afternoon
sartinly	certainly, for certain
saytered	thoroughly soaked
scade	harm; mischief
scamble	to make a confusion of anything
scandalize	to abuse someone
scar	exposed to: 'Our house stands quite scar to the sea.'
scorse	to exchange
scrow	angry; dark and scowling
scud	driving rain; mist
seraphim	a barrel-organ in a church
shackle	to idle about, to waste time; to be very busy about nothing
shacklebreeches	a slow, lazy person
shacky	shabby; ragged
shatter	a unspecific amount, number or quantity: 'There's a tidy shatter of hops this year.'
Sheeres	the Shires; anywhere beyond Sussex and Kent – sheereman
sheereway	a bridleway
shepherd's crown	a fossil sea-urchin found in chalk

A Sussex man poses in his round frock

WUNT BE DRUV!

shim	a glimpse of something
short	out of temper; unable to give a civil answer
shruck	shrieked
shuck	to shell peas; to undress
shuckish	(of weather) unsettled
skice	to run quickly and slily so as to avoid detection
skivel/skiver	a skewer
skreel	to scream; a scream
slabby	dirty; wet and slippery; greasy
slack	loose conversation
slap	in good condition; hearty
slummocky	messy; untidy
sniggler	a light frost
snob	a travelling shoemaker; a cobbler
snudge	to hold down the head; to walk as if in deep thought
snuffy	angry
sodger	(literally = soldier) a red herring
solly	a tottering or unstable condition: 'all of a solly'
some-one-time	now and then; occasionally
somewhen	sometime
soodling	the act of strolling about
soor	exclamation expressing surprise
soss about	to mix different things together, particularly liquids
spannel about	to make a mess; to make dirty fooprints on a floor
sprackish	smart and active
sprug up	neatly dressed
spry	cheerful, lightsome
spud	a hole in a sock where the foot shows through
squimbly	feeling unwell or upset
stean	to pave a road with stones
still	quiet; respectable: 'He's a nice still man.'
stived up	crowded
stiver about	to stagger

stomachy	proud; obstinate
stood	stuck fast
stride	a long distance
strives	rivalry
stupe	stupid; dull
suddent	suddenly
suent	pleasant; agreeable
sullage	filth or dirt
sushy	in want of water
Sussex moon	a man sent on ahead with a lantern fastened behind him
Sussex swede	an ignorant rustic
swanky	light beer. Also called **swipes**
sweal	to singe or burn; to scour (clothes)
swelt	hot; faint
swinge	to flog
swish	a stick; a switch
swymy	giddy, faint
talk thin	to talk in a low voice
tan flawing	the act of taking the bark off trees
tell	to count
tempersome	quick tempered
tessy	angry
that time of day	in those days
thro	from – to and thro
tightish	in good health
timmersome	timid
tinker	to mend something clumsily
tip-tongued	having an affected manner of speaking
tissick	a slight, tickling cough
to and agin	backwards and forwards
took-to	ashamed; vexed
tooter	a seaside trader
to rights	completely, perfectly

t'other day	the day before yesterday
tramp	gin and water
truck	rubbish; odds and ends
trull	to bowl a hoop
turn	occasion; '*I was along there one turn.*'
twort	pert and saucy
tye	a common; a large open field
unaccountable	exceedingly
utchy	cold
valiant	stout; well-built
wapsey	spiteful; waspish
weeze	to ooze
whapple way	a bridle way through fields or woods
whiffle	to come in gusts
whist	silent
wild, the	the weald
willocky	madly angry
windshaken	thin; puny; weak
winterproud	cold
wrockled	wrinkled
yape	to gossip
yetner	not nearly: *i be'ant forty year old yetner*

FISHY LANGUAGE

The fishermen of Sussex, now much reduced in number, had their own way of talking – specialized words and idioms, and even a distinctive intonation.

backstay/backster	a wide, flat board, strapped to the feet by fishermen for walking over loose beach or soft mud on the seashore. Also called **cleat board**
beach	shingle brought from the sea-coast as opposed to inland gravel

bending-in day   the start of the mackerel season at Brighton

boco   a large quantity (from French *beaucoup*, a term used by fishermen in eastern Sussex)

buss   a short, heavy and very strong fishing boat characteristic of Hastings and used in the off-season as a trader

Some 'chop-backs', 1908

chop back   a Hastings fisherman (a derogatory term)

chucle   a triangular frame used to support the bilge-keep of a beached boat, also called **squat**

cleat board   see *backstay*

clopper/clog boot   a boot with a wooden sole, worn by fishermen on some parts of the coast

cock   a small boat used in the herring fishery

dab   a flounder

dark   a night when the moon does not appear, a term used by sailors, especially smugglers

deese/deeze   a place where herrings are dried. Also called **herring-hang**

doling   a fishing boat with two masts

doss/dorsel   one of a pair of panniers in which fish are carried on a horse

draw net   a fishing net pulled through the water by two men

egger-nogger   sleet

fare   a period during which certain kinds of fishing took place

flapper   a piece of wood which the fishermen strap over their boots for walking on shingle

flew   a kind of fishing net

flewar/flewer   a boat used in herring fishery

harbour duck/harbour shark
    Rye harbour man

haviler/heaver	a crab
hempshare/hemshare	land in Brighton used by fishing families for growing hemp to make ropes
herring-hang	See *deese*
hog boat/hoggie	a big, tubby fishing boat peculiar to Brighton
hovelling	the act of taking any pickings which might be had from ships in distress, an ancient longshore-seafaring occupation
jug	a Brighton fisherman
kellick	an anchor
keveling	(in Brighton) the skate
messenger	a white cloud driven by the wind. Also called windog
mudlark	a Rye fisherman
noward	a peculiar kind of net, comparatively short and very deep
ore	seaweed washed on shore by the tides
pandle	a shrimp
planet	(in Hastings) a brief and sudden gale – planety, *adj.*
pork bolter	a Worthing fisherman
port boy	a small low cloud in a clear sky
prickle	a fish basket which holds a bushel
punt	a Hastings open-decked fishing boat
rake	the action of the sea when it breaks on the shore with a long grating sound
rann	a measure of netting
ripier	a man from the coast who carries baskets of fish to inland towns and villages
salt	a marsh near the sea which is overflowed by the tides
sean/seine	a very large net used for catching mackerel or herrings
shotnett fair	the period, extending from mid-April to June, when mackerel are fished
siever	the total catch of fish at one tide
squat	See **chucle**

stade	a shore where ships are beached, as at Hastings
swallocky	(in a spell of hot weather) cloudy, presaging a thunder storm; wet and windy
tachener	a young man employed on a fishing boat
truggy	(of weather) bad, dirty
warp	four herrings
windog	See **messenger**

COUNTRY MATTERS

The population was far less concentrated in towns in days gone by, so that most people brought up in Sussex were familiar with the countryside all about them. They used a great many words which have totally disappeared from the language.

adder's meat	greater stitchwort
adder's spear	a large dragonfly
ad(d)ling his shoon	(of a horse rolling in pasture) earning his shoes
affut	a newt
agarve	a May berry
aigarce	a haw
ale hoof/alliff	ground ivy
amendment	manure
ammut caste	an ant-hill. Also **emmet caste**
andring	the sport of hunting squirrels on St Andrew's Day
apple-pie	great hairy willowherb
appleterre	an orchard
applety	a loft where apples are stored
apse	an aspen tree
arder	an adder
ark	a triangular chicken house which originated in Sussex

assart	land cleared of woodland on which rents could be paid
bagged up	(of a cow) taken to market with a full udder so as to appear a larger milker than she really is
bait	afternoon refreshment in the hay and harvest field
bargeboat	the green woodpecker. Also called **galleybird, gallowsbird, yaffle**
barrel	the round part of the hook of a shepherd's crook
batfowler	one who takes birds at night using a large, folding net on long poles
beepot/beeve	a beehive
beeskep	a beehive, especially one made of straw
bennets	long grass that bends in the wind
bilbo	a sheep bow; a v-shaped wooden frame to hold a sheep's head during shearing, clipping or trimming
binding/bondcord	manilla yarn used to tie up sacks of corn
bine	the hop stalk which binds round the pole
Bishop Barnaby	a ladybird
black ram night	a sheep shearers' celebration
blindworm	a slow-worm
bostal/borstal	a pathway up a hill, especially on escarpment of the Sussex Downs
bottom	a downland valley
brake	bracken
briffens	See *cavings*
brish	to trim a hedge: brishings = clippings; brisher = hedger
brock	(1) the badger, (2) the froghopper
brook	a water meadow
bud	a calf in the first year; by extension, a stupid fellow (also buddy)
bullock	a fat beast of either sex

A bargeboat

bullock leaze	the right to turn cattle out on a common to graze
bussick	a hassock
butter and eggs	bird's-foot trefoil. Also called (among other common names) **God Almighty's thumbs and fingers** and **ladies' fingers**
buzzing clock	a cockchafer
caffinch/caffincher	the chaffinch
cats' tails	the male blossom of hazel or willow
cavings	the short straws or ears removed from the corn when it is threshed. Also called **briffens**
chee	a hen roost
chequer	the wild service tree
churn owl	the nightjar
clavel	one of the individual grains in an ear of wheat
clodbird	the corn bunting
close	a farmyard
cluck/clucket	a long and narrow sheep bell
coop	a T-shaped cutting in the turf to trap wheatears
copson	a fence placed on top of a small dam to keep sheep from crossing a ditch
cord	a pile of wood cut up for burning
cordbat	a stack of large pieces of wood
crack nut	a hazel nut
crowsfoot	the buttercup
culver	a pigeon or dove
cutty	the wren. Also called **juggy, kitty, scutty**
dabbie/dabchick	the moorhen
deaf adder	the slow-worm
deal	a sow's nipple
dencher	garden waste burnt slowly and used to improve the soil
dogger	a support for the shafts of a cart
dolly dishwasher	the pied wagtail

doole	(on the Downs) a conical lump of earth raised to show the bounds of parishes or farms
dowels	levels; low marshes in which the water lies in winter
drat/draw	a squirrel's nest
driftway	a cattle path to water; a greenway
drink	liquid medicine for cattle
drove road	an unenclosed road through a farm leading to different fields; a greenway
dumbledore	the humble bee or bumblebee
dwair	a strong cross-bar in the floor of a waggon
earsh	a field of stubble. Also called **gratten**

A dumbledore

effet/eft	a newt
egga	a berry or haw
ellar/ellet/eller	an elder tree. Also eller
ellum	an elm – elven, *adj.*
erne	a heron
ether	a hedge. Also **edder**
eve-jar	the nightjar
fag/fog	(1) last season's grass (2) to cut corn or stubble close to the ground
fanner/fanner hawk	
	a kestrel
flap	a large, broad mushroom
flapjack	a sort of tart made of apples in a thin piece of paste. Also called **apple turnover**
fleck	the fur of hares or rabbits
flindermouse/flittermouse	
	a bat
flop	a net for catching rabbits

fly golding	a ladybird. Also called **God Almighty's cow, Lady Anne, ladycow**
fold tare/fold tail	the improvement in land resulting from sheep having been folded on it
fordrough	a cattle track to water; a grass ride; a drove road
forestall/fostel	the house and buildings of a farm with non-arable land
futtice	a weasel
galleybird/gallowsbird	See *bargeboat*
gate	a farmyard
gazel	a berry, especially a blackcurrant
gold cup/goldilocks	the buttercup
grandfather	a daddy-long-legs
grandmother's nightcap	the white campion
grandmother's pincushion	the field scabious
gratten	See *earsh*
greybird	the mistle thrush. Also called **storm cock**
guess sheep	a young ewe that has been with the ram and had no lambs
gull	(1) a gosling (2) willow blossom
haffer/harfer	a heifer
hagtrack	a circle of coarse green grass, supposed to be the tracks of witches that have danced there at night
headache	the corn poppy
heal	to cover
heave gate	a low gate so constructed as to lift out from the posts rather than opening with hinges
hedge-pick /hedge-mike	the dunnock or hedge sparrow
hemmel	a fold
hogpound	a pigsty. Also called **pigscot**

hornicle	hornet. Also called **humbledore**
horsebeach/husbeech	
	the hornbeam
hover	(of soil) light and friable
humble cow	a cow without horns
humbledore	See **hornicle**
hurt	a whortleberry or bilberry
hyme	a wasps' or wild bees' nest, etc.
jack	a heron
jack abbler	the crested newt
jack in prison	love-in-a-mist
jack-in-the-hedge	the red campion
jacob	the jackdaw
juggy	(1) See **cutty**. (2) a squirrel
jump-up-and-kiss-me	
	the pansy. Also **kiss me**
june bug	the green beetle or rose beetle
just beast/joist beast	
	a beast taken in to graze
keck	cow parsley
kid	a pea or bean pod
kime/kine	the weasel
kind	(of beasts) fat; doing well
kips	the common tern
lades	rails which project round the top of a waggon to enable it to carry a greater load. Compare **raves**
ladies' fingers	See **butter and eggs**
lag-a-long	a long, narrow marshy meadow
laine	an open tract of arable land on, or at the foot of, the Downs
laylock	a lilac bush
loggerhead	a tadpole
long purples	the early purple orchid

A 'jack' or an 'erne'

A kips

merry tree	the wild cherry
milkmaid	the cuckooflower or lady's smock
moonshiner	a beast that will not fatten
naughty man's plaything	the stinging nettle
old man's nightcap	bindweed (*Convolvulus sepium*). Also called **piddlepot**
owlet	a moth
ox-steddle	a stall for oxen
parson rook	the hooded crow
pat	a pig trough
pickle	pitchfork
pigeon cove	a dovecote
pilrag	a field that has been dug up and neglected
plaw	a small wood
poad milk	the first milk produced by a cow after calving
poke	a long sack
pop hole	an unnetted bolt-hole covered by a dog during rabbit-catching
poults	beans and peas sown and harvested together
pug	(1) a kind of loam (2) a ferret
raves	a framework fitted onto a cart to accommodate an extra load

Oxen at Work in Sussex.

reynolds/Mus Reynolds
    the fox

rife — a ditch on moorland

ringle — to put a ring in a pig's snout

rowens/roughings — the coarse grass which grows after mowing and is left for cattle to eat in the winter. Compare **fag/fog**

sheere mouse — the field mouse

sow waps — a queen wasp

speens/spenes — the teats of a cow

stopples — deep footmarks made by cattle or horses

strig — the stalk of any fruit or flower

sungreen — the house-leek

Sussex weed — an oak tree

tater dog — the caterpillar or pupa of the death's head hawk moth

tea leaf — a siskin

teg leaze — the right to turn out one sheep to feed on a common

teeler — a piece of wood used in a rabbit trap to keep the wire in place

thwartle — to cross-plough

voller — a fallow field

webbing — the practice of rabbiting with a long net

weeson — throat

willick — a guillemot

winterpick — a sloe

wuffling — the turning of hay after cutting

WORKING LIFE

Downland shepherds used to count their sheep in pairs with strange incantations. One variation ran 'one-erum, two-erum, cockerum, shue-erum, shitherum, shatherum, wine-berry, wagtail, tarrydiddle, den.' (So den was twenty.) The language has gone, and so have the ancient, old-time shepherds with their weather-beaten faces and their large umbrellas to keep off both sun and rain, but at least there are still a few flocks of sheep on Sussex hills which were once covered white as snow with them. Other trades and occupations have disappeared altogether, including the iron industry, which flourished in the Weald from the 16th century and clung on into the 19th.

Sheep-washing in Sussex c.1900s

ancony	a **bloom** of iron
bagging-bill/-hook	
	See **fag hook**
barking iron	See **flawing spud**
barley champter	an implement for cutting off the beards of barley
bay	a pond-head or dam to keep in store water, as for the Sussex iron industry
bellus	bellows
billhook	a sharp cutting tool, hooked at the end, used for pruning and for tapering the points of spiles
bloom	a mass of wrought iron
bloomery	a placewhere wrought iron was made.
bout	a day's work
bristlebat	See **rubber**

broom clisher	a broom maker
broom dasher	a dealer in faggots, brooms, etc
bristle-bat	a stone for sharpening a scythe
bunny	a wooden or brick drain laid under a road or gateway. Also called **cocker**
bunter	a machine formery used for cleaning corn
burner	a charcoal maker. Also **collier**, a later term
busheler	a tallyman who measured hops from the bin
canister	a type of sheep bell, the most common type in Sussex
chafery	the fire of an iron hammer or forge
chip	the wooden part of a plough to which the share was fastened
chogs	the refuse cuttings of hop plants when dressed in the spring before being polled
clat	to cut wool and other matter from a sheep's rear end
clish	the band by which heath or birch brooms are held together

SHEEP-SHEARING.

clocksmith	a watchmaker
cocker	See **bunny**
collier	See **burner**
comb	(1) an implement used by thatchers (2) the ridge of a thatch
costrel	a leather or wooden bottle used by a labourer, especially at harvest
cray ring	the ring on a scythe into which the blade is fixed
densher plough	an implement used for turf-cutting
dezzick/duzzick	a day's work
dog	an implement used by thatchers
elevener	See **'levener**
fag-hook/fagging hook	a hook used for hedge or bush trimming

56

fellmonger	See **tawer**
flake	cleft wood
flaw	to strip bark; to flay
flawing spud	an iron tool with a heart-shaped blade, used for stripping bark from newley felled oak trees. Also called **barking iron**, **tan sput**
folding bar	an iron bar with a broad point and a flattened section on the shaft, used for erecting wattles to fold sheep on the Downs
fore-summer	the top rail in front of a waggon
gaberdine	a loose frock worn by farm labourers
gee-woot!	an expression used by waggoners to make the leading horse go to the off-side.
graff/graffing tool	a curved spade used by drainers
groom	an implement used by thatchers for carrying bundles of straw
handbill	a sharp tool with a short handle used in cutting underwood (sometimes pronounced **anvil**)
hedge carpenter	one who has not been apprenticed to a carpenter and so properly learnt his trade

Loading the waggon c. 1900

hopdog	an implement used to draw hop-poles out of the ground
hop horse	a short ladder used by hop-pickers
joint steddlel	a stool
'levener	a worker's luncheon Also called **levenses, elevener**
lip	a wooden box in which seed was carried for sowing
looker	a shepherd
neb	the handle of a scythe
percer	a punch used by blacksmiths
pitcher	a man who, with the aid of a pitchfork, loads corn or hay onto a waggon
pole puller	a man who pulls the hop-poles out of the ground and lays them down for the pickers
rearing feast	a feast provided for the workmen when the roof is put on a house
rousers	large deafening fireworks let off on November 5th in Lewes
rubber	a whetstone. Also called **bristlebat**
runagate	a good-for-nothing
rusty	unruly; ill-humoured
seedsman	the foreman of a farm whose business it is to do the sowing
shim	a kind of plough with a double blade
spar/sparrer	a twisted stick used by thatchers to secure the straw on the top of a stack or roof of building
statesman	a man who owns a few acres of land and farms them himself
tan sput	See **flawing spud**
tawer	a leather dresser. Also called **fellmonger**
traverse/travase	the place adjoining a blacksmith's shop where horses are shod
tree throwing	the act of felling trees for timber
usage/usuals	provisions given to workmen in addition to their wages

CHAPTER 6

Some Colourful Characters

For every writer creating whole volumes in dialect, there were dozens who attempted to catch the language of real Sussex-characters in works that were otherwise written in standard English. Inevitably there is a 'local yokel' flavour to much of this, since these authors spoke otherwise themselves and were well aware that they were capturing a dying tongue that was by then largely the preserve of the uneducated and untravelled.

Bob Copper, a member of a famous singing family and the author of several wonderful books, had much less of a leap to make than most. He grew up speaking the dialect and always respected the people who spoke it, however much he had learned to 'talk proper' for the sake of the world outside his native Rottingdean. Here's a memory from his book *Early to Rise*. He and his father are watching a hare.

''E's makin' f'garden bushes,' said Dad. 'See that bank over there, jest past the bushes alongside the shepherd's 'ut? Me an' ol' Teddy Sherfold dug three badgers out there on Sunday aft'noon when we was shepherd boys. You 'member ol' Teddy, dun't ye? 'E was a rare ol' sportsman, 'e was. Flick, feather or fin, boy, 'e didn't care what it was s'long as 'e 'ad a bit o' sport. I couldn't stick 'is missus though, she was a tartar. If she'd 'a' bin the only girl in the world an' I'd 'a' bin the only boy, like in the song, wal, that'd 'a' bin the end o' the 'uman race, I dun't mind tellin' ye.

'You know one night ol' Teddy 'ad a bit of a ding-dong down the Royal Oak an' 'e didn't get 'ome till about ar' past two in the morning. 'E undresses quiet like, so as not to wake 'er up, an' was standin' there in 'is shirt an' jest as 'e cocks one leg up an' sits on the edge o' the bed she turns over, opens one eye an' says, "Wherever are you going to at this time of the morning, Ted?" Wal, ol' Teddy was pretty often up in middlin' time t' catch the tide for a bit o' fishing and 'e didn't want t' upset 'er, so 'e says, "Prawnin', dear." An' 'e puts 'is clothes back on, went out an' spent the rest

o' the night in the shed at the bottom o' the garden. 'E would 'a' gone prawnin', look, only 'e couldn't – the tide was in.'

Barclay Wills, born in London in 1877, came to Sussex in the 1920s and became so familiar with the downland shepherds that he wrote several books about them, among them *Shepherds of Sussex*.

This shepherd is singularly particular in his dislike of female visitors to his lambing-fold. Once he said to me: 'Boss's wife be too fond o' poken' 'bout here. If I got a ewe as wants a doctor I fastens t'wattle tight. I wunt have women lookin' on while I be doctor, fur 't'int decent!'

One of his experiences of lambing time is worth recording. He was working for a gentleman farmer, and had entire charge of the sheep, but at lambing time the owner came to look at the fold and found him attending to a ewe that was ill and very weak. ('Twur a biggish place, an' he wur a real genelman, you unnerstan', explained the shepherd.) The farmer was very sorry for the ewe and said: 'Can nothing be done for her, shepherd?' and my friend replied: 'Yes, 'twould be a great help to her if you could give her some gruel and a good dose of whisky in it.' The boss smiled at such a request. He had never attended to sick sheep. 'Well, John,' he said, 'if you really mean it, she shall have it!' 'I certainly do mean it,' replied old John, 'though I s'pose you be thinkin' as I be arter a drop 'o whisky, but I bean't, an' if I had any I'd give it to t'ewe.' Soon the boss departed

Shepherds with their flock near Clayton windmill, in the early 20th century

60

and after an interval the shepherd was visited by a stately butler, who appeared with a tray, on which rested a large bowl of gruel and two tumblers of whisky!

Nancy Price, a journalist and author, lived in West Sussex and published *Jack by the Hedge* in 1942. In the chapter 'The Devil Defaults' she meets a heavily whiskered tramp:

"Ad me raison, bein' 'ere'.
'I'm curious'.
He regarded me with twinkling blue eyes from under the brim of his disreputable old hat. 'Wimmin moastly be'.
'You won't tell me, then?'
'Thur be nawthin' secret as I knaws on – it's they fleases, an' they cooms off lik' water on a duck's back i' bracken; nawthin' lik' a doss down i' bracken wen 'ee be troubled wi' likes o' they. Thur be them as can stand 'em, but I rackons as I allus 'ad out-o'-way itchy skin'.
I stepped back instinctively as he shook himself; then he sniffed appreciatively. 'Purty marnin', thaat's sartin. I'll be 'ome afore sundown. I ba'ent a feller as sleeps reg'lar under 'edges, or slinks to wark'us fur a doss. I gat a 'ome oop ower yander an' I doos a liddle stone-breakin', an I doos a liddle crow-skeerin' – thirsty wark, I tell 'ee'.
He spat, and looked at my thermos hopefully.
'Not a drop of coffee left, I'm afraid', I said.
'They fancy drinkses ba'ent to my likin'. Drap o' cider, a gin 'ot, or a pint o' beer, an' I wunt say no'.

Readers of the *West Sussex Gazette* will be familiar with Lilian Ramsey's columns, written from 1936 until shortly before her death in 1974 (and often reprinted since) under the pseudonym 'A Sussex woman' – which she wasn't, as it happens. They feature the relationship of a gentlewoman with her Sussex-speaking charwoman, Mrs Paddick. Here's the column dated August 25, 1936:

'I've never known fruit so scarce as it is this year, Mrs Paddick', I said. 'Nobody seems to have got any'.
'Them two furriners up at Wincels have got a nice shatter of apples on their trees', replied Mrs Paddick. 'But they're unaccountable deedy. Apples is very platty this year'.
The 'furriners' at Wincels are two spinsters, retired gardeners, who have annoyed the village very much by pursuing their own methods of growing

things. When they took over Wincels, an old cottage that has stood empty for four years, with a garden full of 'rubbidge', they 'aksed ol Exwhyzed' to dig it up for them.

'Wanted me to pull out all the rubbidge,' he grumbled to his friends. 'I always digs 'em in, I told 'em. That's how we do's it in West Sussex. It's as good as amendment for the ground.

'But no, they would have it all out an' lay the kecksies an' lily on one side an' bury all the other rubbidge along o' some stuff as they bought at the chymist's. I told 'em they'd better dig it theirsens, an' off I went.'

Later in the spring passers-by 'squinnied' over the hedge and saw the 'furriners' digging a trench and planting potatoes at the bottom. One old man obligingly called across to them: 'That ain't the way to plant yer taters, ain't you got a debber? I'll give you the lent o' mine.' But they refused in their 'tip-tongued' way and went on planting in a trench.

One night their nearest neighbour, Mrs A, woke them up to ask them to telephone for the doctor as her baby was in convulsion. One of them got up to render first-aid and found that the baby had been given pear juice.

Mrs Paddick explained the reason to me. 'If you was longin' for something before the baby came you gives the baby pear juice if 'twas fruit an' rabbits brains if 'twas meat.

'But that Miss Addle, she rounded on Mrs A, as she told her you dedn't ought to give babies nothin' but milk. An' she, as never been married, learnin' Mrs A to bring up a baby!'

The two spinsters continued unconcernedly to garden according to their own methods. They sowed their garden peas one at a time in cartons and planted them out, so that they had peas before anyone else in the village.

I asked old Exwhyzed today how his potatoes were looking.

'Blighted like everyone else's,' he replied shortly. ' 'Ceptin' them deedy furriners up at Wincels. Their taters looks fine. I s'spose they're not so such down there as we are. Tarrible sushy our gardens are. But they've got a nice shatter of apples an' pears, an' their taters looks unaccountable fine. Luck, I s'spose, for it's not the way they planted 'em!'

CHAPTER 7

Folk Singing and the Dialect Today

Read the words of a folk song on the page and you won't be aware of much dialect, but hear a singer of the old school tackle it with the appropriate accent, intonation and stress and you're transported back to the day before yesterday, when pubs all over the county rang to the sound of traditional music.

Annie Onslow, born in 1916, remembers her very first job, working at the Royal Oak pub in High Hurstwood. This was in the early 1930s.

'To hear those farmers that come in, hear them talking broad Sussex, and singing,' she says wistfully. 'They used to sing some old songs. They were really old and you wouldn't hear them now at all. Lovely songs! Each man had his own, and he'd sit and sing it. The man that used to mend the shoes – the snob – he used to have his song, "Poor Little Joe".

'They sang when they felt like it, and when they had a little too much drink, I suppose – also when there was a share-out of the slate club. They paid in each week and if anyone was sick they used to give them a little from that slate club. And they used to have a sing-song when there was a share-out of it.

'Some of them would join in the chorus, I think, but not many. I don't know where they got their tunes from, because they never played anything. They used to sing the tune. Mostly they were old farmers, but they were good really – lovely songs. Course, there wasn't no women ever went in there much. Not in those days.'

Then Annie remembers one of the songs and sings it to me in a sweet voice:

> *What is the life of a man any more than the leaves?*
> *A man has his seasons, so why should he grieve?*
> *Although in this wide world he appears bright and gay,*
> *Like the leaves we shall wither and soon fade away.*

Bob Lewis, a noted Sussex folk singer, confirms the idea of song ownership.

'There was an interesting formality. I tend to observe it, too. If a song was somebody's song, and you were in company, you wouldn't sing that song because it was regarded as being theirs – "Old so-and-so always sings that song" – not a written law, but a kind of courtesy. I learned a lot of my songs from my mother. She had amazing recall: 'Pretty Ploughboy' she'd sing.

'My songs? Where do I start? *Sussex Pig*, *Sweet Country Life*, *Three Old Crows* – I got that one from old Alfie Ainger, who was landlord of the Royal Oak at Hooksway, Midhurst way. He was the oldest licensee in Sussex, and he ran this very primitive pub (no spirits, just beer and cider) until the late 1960s.'

Bob Lewis at the Tramps' Supper, the Fox, Charlton, 1976

Three old crows sat on a tree,
They were as black as black could be,
Old thing.

Said one black crow unto his mates
Where shall we go for food to ate
Old thing?

Bob was born in 1936 and saw the tradition disappearing.

'There was a change in the villages after the last war. There were a lot of incomers who took the pubs, and there were people arriving from the colonies, ex-colonial types who thought "This is going to be my personal pub and I'll have all my gin and tonic friends in." The locals were a little bit squeezed out, and in quite a lot of cases they were discouraged. And they were certainly discouraged from singing.

FOLK SINGING AND THE DIALECT TODAY

'I went with three mates of mine to the Bat and Ball at Hambledon, over the Hampshire border. We were having a few pints and there were some locals in there, so we started to have a bit of a sing-song. And this tweedy looking woman came over and shouted at the top of her voice: "No singing in here!" So we downed our pints and went to another pub down the road!

'I know about 250 songs and 75 per cent of them come from Sussex. There was 800 songs they reckon come from Sussex alone.'

The first folk song revival was in the early years of the 20th century, when Cecil Sharp, Ralph Vaughan Williams and other members of the English Folk Song Society went round the country collecting the words and tunes from local people. Shirley Collins, a singer well known to everyone in the English folk world (let alone Sussex), came in on the second wave, in which Bob Lewis also played a major part.

Shirley Collins in the 1960s

'In the fifties the folk scene was opening up,' she recalls. 'There was a folk revival, a new interest in folk music, and I travelled all over the country – literally – singing at various folk clubs. There were concerts, and universities would have their folk clubs, too. I was supposed to be a teacher, but I wanted to be a singer. I wanted to sing folk songs because I'd learned some at home and I loved them.

'Then the BBC used to have a series called 'Country Magazine' and 'As I Rode Out', and I used to listen to this stuff because it had field recordings. I heard the Copper family on there, and it was music I absolutely loved. I think one of the reasons I've ended up poor was because I just sang this music. There wasn't a huge living to be made out of it, but I managed to do that right up until I was forty-something. There are so many real Sussexsongs: *Bonny Labouring Boy, Sweet Primroses, Sweep Chimney Sweep* ...

Now here I do stand with my hoe all in my hand
Like a soldier that's on the sentery (repeat)
I will work for a better sort, I will work for a better sort
And kindly thank them for it.
I will work, work, work and I'll work
And I'll work for none but gentery.

'When I sang, my accent used to get that little bit broader. If you're singing folk songs and southern England songs and you make it too "naice", as if you're a proper singer, you sound ridiculous. They have to be sung in the voice that people spoke in. And so my singing was always an extension of my speech, and perhaps those *a* sounds got a bit wider.'

Foremost among Sussex singers are the Copper family, who have a worldwide reputation. Bob Copper, who died in 2004 in his late eighties, kept the tradition alive in both his singing and his evocative writing, and his children John and Jill are perpetuating it, with their own children performing, too: the seventh generation.

'What's remarkable,' says John Copper, 'is that Bob remembered his grandfather saying that this was how he heard the song sung in his own grandfather's lifetime. That takes us right back to the 18th century. Of course there'll have been some other influences creeping in, but there's nowhere else that you'll find such a long, unbroken tradition of English folk music.'

The fifties' revival was more pronounced in Sussex than in most other parts of England, Vic Smith explains. Although not a

Vic Smith

FOLK SINGING AND THE DIALECT TODAY

Sussex man himself, Vic has been a leading figure in the county folk scene for many years and has an overview of the subject second to none.

'Suddenly there were all these twenty-somethings coming to pubs and folk clubs. The genuine old singers – people like George Belton, George Spicer and Bob Blake – found it very strange that the young people thought what they had was important. The Copper family were prominent, of course, but they were only the tip of the iceberg.

'It happened in the Weald most of all. If you went to the Cherry Tree in Copthorne or the Stone Quarry in Chelwood Gate on a Saturday night you were much more likely than not to hear singing. The Plough at Tilgate and the Royal Oak in Newick were popular, too. In fact, most rural pubs in Wealden Sussex had some singing, and there was a network: people heard by word of mouth where the singing would be, and off they'd go by motorbikes and sidecars.

'You could say that the singing is a formalized way of maintaining dialect, but it's part of a wider tradition that includes broom dances and step dancing. Dancing was particularly associated with hop-picking in the east of the county, and it survived into the fifties in pubs. I still call and play for dances virtually every Saturday, with my wife playing concertina.

'And then there were the stories. The old guys would tell the ones their parents told them, and they'd almost unconsciously adopt the accent and choice of words that their parents would have had: "When we come through the lych on the way to church", rather than "gate". It's part of a richness that celebrates the old way. The songs have been a bit more tenacious perhaps, but there are still traditional stories around.'

Bob Lewis has a remarkable tale of his own to tell, concerning a favourite yarn in Sussex pubs – the story about Lord Leconfield's lost sheep.

'This was one of the best-known jokes in Sussex for years, and everybody across the length and breadth of Sussex knew this story. This is how it goes:

Lord Leconfield, he had this flock of sheep and he lost 'em. Now they got some detective chaps from London, and they come round asking if anybody knew about these here sheep, and one of these fellows comes into the local. And at that time o' day if anyone strange came into the pub everyone went quiet and nobody said a word, like. And this chap says, 'Look, Lord Leconfield has lost his sheep and does anyone know anything about it?' Nobody didn't say nothing, so he tried again.

And there's an old gaffer sat up under the chimney, like. He says, 'I know who 'ad 'em.' So this detective says to him, 'Look here my man, you'd better

tell me what you knows about this.' And he says to him, 'Well it ought to be worth a pint of beer didn't it?' With reluctance like he bought the old feller a pint of beer and he said, 'Well now you'd better tell me what you know about it, then.'

'Oh,' the old feller says, 'it's like this 'ere.' He says, 'Old Lord Leconfield, 'e 'ad' em. But he in't got 'em now, 'as he?!'

'There was always that sort of London people come down to Sussex who would take the mickey,' Bob says, 'but Sussex people were just as good taking the rise the other way. But the interesting thing about this story was that it was an ancient political joke. I found that out completely by accident.

'I was in the rare book bit of the library foraging about, and I found a newspaper account of a Sussex election in 1820. It was the most lurid report. There were about three weeks of free beer, food and drink in Chichester. One of the people involved was Colonel Wyndham of Petworth Park, who was one of the illegitmate children of the Earl of Egremont – he had 23 of them.

'The landowners was always backing one side or the other, Whigs or Tories, and if old Lord Leconfield at Petworth said my candidate is So-and-So he expected all his tenants to vote for him and do exactly as they were told. And the joke was really about this, because there were two speeches. One was about the lost sheep and how they'd been decoyed away by the other lot – lurid language about ravenous wolves – and the next day the opposite camp made this speech about the lost sheep being found: Baaa! Most amazing. The joke was about the people who raised their fingers at him and voted the way they wanted.

'The story stuck, and it was still current in the 1950s, more than 130 years later, although the political origins of it had been entirely lost. When I read that it was like someone giving me an electric shock.'

The disappearance of the Sussex dialect has been predicted for the past two hundred years, but today it is unmistakably in its death throes. Within a generation surelye, there will be only a tinge of an accent on a few ancient tongues to remind us that it was once a vigorous local language with its own idioms and vocabulary.

The following interviews are an attempt to record its very last traces. By the time my contributors were growing up, the dialect had been infiltrated from all sides, but it was, for all that, still something sufficiently distinct from received pronunciation to be frowned upon and ironed out, by school masters and mistresses. Thank goodness they didn't entirely succeed.

Dorothy Willliams (2nd left) with her family in Telham.
Fred is on the left.

'Oi oosed to spake like thaat when Oi lived at Telham', Dorothy Williams tells me, the accent readily springing to her lips as if she were a young girl again. She was born Dorothy Ball, in 1912, and lived at Telham, near Battle, until she was eight years old. Her older brother Fred wrote an evocative account of their growing up, *A Breath of Fresh Air*.

Their father, also Fred, worked as a gardener at 'the big house' at a time when the entire population of the tiny hamlet numbered around thirty. There were the Balls, the Ticehursts and the Turleys.

'Old Ted Turley, he was a farmer's son. They'd farmed there for two or three hundred years, and he was very very broad Sussex. We'd all got the flu – I suppose it must have been 1918 – and all we had left at the door was a pint of skimmed milk. Nobody would come past the door. If they left anything it was on the doorstep. And nobody could go and fetch it, because we were all in bed with the flu. Ted opened the door and said "Foun' nes' marnin', Fred, fower heggs".

Isn't that lovely! He was saying "Found a nest this morning, Fred – four eggs." When I went to work in a shop, ages after, we all had numbers. My friend was 10 and I was 44, and I used to say "fowety fower".

'You've no idea how cut off we were from the villages. I remember when we went home from school once a week, there used to be a large coach drawn by four horses and it would stand on Battle Green, the Abbey green, and the driver would stand shouting "Fairlight, Lover's Seat, Battle Abbey once a week." And I used to wonder what Fairlight was like. I mean it was a foreign land to me. I only knew Battle and Crow'urst when I was at Telham. Everything was a foreign country. You didn't get many visitors. If you got a stranger in, all the kids would follow them. Nobody could commit any crimes there; they never had a bit of peace to themselves.'

She recalls singing for Alan Lomax, one of the great folk song collectors. This is what she sang:

As I rode out one May morning
All in a blooming spring
I overheard a maid complain
And grievous did she sing.

How cruel were her pari-ents
They did her so annoy
They would not let her marry with
Her bonny labouring boy

It was her secondary education that took the Sussex off Dorothy's tongue, except for special occasions, of course.

'I went to school in Hastings and the teacher made fun of me. She wouldn't listen to what I said until I changed my accent. Where she'd come from, I don't know as to why she should be so fussy. I thought they should encourage your dialect, not knock it out, but that was the thing then I suppose.'

But recall of the dialect comes back in an instant.

'We had our *a*s long, didn't we? And we were always having a dose of something – a dose of bad weather, a dose of someone grumbling at us, a dose of school – everything was a dose.

'We used to use words like *chavee* because there were gypsies around periodically, and that meant a gypsy boy. And *mush* was also a gypsy word, which mum didn't like us using. We used to call one another *mush*. If she heard it, she'd correct us.

'A fox was always Reynard or Mr Tod. And Mr Denyer always called the moon Phoebe. He was a widower, and, as he always looked up in the sky, I thought that was his dead wife's name, Phoebe.

'We'd talk about Battle *girt 'ood* (for wood), where there were *wo'ak* trees, and each one would be an *ooge girt* thing. A *point* was a pint and joints were *jints*. *Puggled* meant puzzled or faintly looney.

'Dad taught us the names of stars: the *girt* plough, the *liddle* plough and the *sodger*. It's got three stars for a belt, three stars for a sword and three stars for a cocked hat. The hunter they call it now. We didn't know such posh names as Orion. The quarter moon was a sickle.

'A *timber tug* was a waggon drawn by horses for pulling the timber out of the wood. We used to see them when we came home from school, and we used to try to hang on the back and get dragged up Battle Hill. They had long whips and the bloke would whip round the back at us.'

Getting a few of the 'good ol' boys' together is a sure way of bringing out the stories, the words and turns of phrase. I sat down at a farmhouse kitchen table in West Sussex with three of them, and heard some great tales of poaching, rabbiting, farming and woodcraft, which are, alas, too long for these pages. I doubt that you'd find more than a few dozen such 'dialect-wise' people throughout the county today.

They were all, of course, raised in the country: it would be impossible to find a 'townie' with a genuine Sussex accent these days. Bob Lomas has the faintest accent of the three, although he can produce the genuine article gloriously at will. Born in 1934, he grew up on a farm at Sullington, but went soldiering for ten years before returning to various kinds of agricultural work.

Ray Chris, born in the same year at Christ's Hospital, spent his formative years on a farm at Oakwood Hill on the Surrey border. Apart from two years as a professional rabbit catcher, he spent his entire working life on farms, which accounts for the fact that he still has the accent and a few of the words.

As we talked it became apparent that the slight seniority of Harvey Stenning, who was born in 1928 at the little hamlet of Bedham, north of Fittleworth, was crucial in dialect terms. Harvey recalls a rural childhood which included working in West Sussex coppices with his father and grandfather, who made pales. During National Service, which took him to northern Italy and Palestine, he found his accent derided – 'I was the only country boy there. I used to have to knuckle up to one or two of them, like' – but he never lost it. Harvey still says

Left to right: Ray Chris, Bob Lomas, Harvey Stenning

'fadder' and 'wid', and, I'm sure, uses more of the old words in his everyday speech. We fell to talking about such matters.

Harvey: If somebody wants directions, I say 'You go across there *caterwise*.' That's diagonal. I very often use that. There are a couple of other words I often say to my wife which my father and grandfather used. In those days, before the war, you never used to go out anywhere of a Sunday. You'd go for a walk and see if you could a find a dinner or so forth – a rabbit or a pheasant. And very often you'd hear 'Where bin 'day, then?' and the reply would be 'Oh, I just wen' *soodlin'* up round Poke's Bottom, had a *scoon about* an' come back 'ome'. *Soodling's* a slow walk, and to *scoon* about is to look about you.

Bob: Tell you a word you don't hear now, and it was always used when I was a boy: *yourn*. It's yourn, not mine.

Harvey: When we were working in the woods we used an axe, a framesaw and a handbill, which properly is a hand billhook. For cutting grass we used a scythe or a faghook.

FOLK SINGING AND THE DIALECT TODAY

Ray: We always called it a *swap*.

Bob: It varied with different places. We all used a scythe much the same everywhere. For cutting grass, we used a swaphook. It had a crank on the handle, otherwise you'd hit your knuckles on the ground. A sickle is straight out, because you cut well above the ground and leave stubble. It can be small, but a sickle doesn't have a crank. A faghook doesn't have a crank on it, but it's heavier because it's got to cut hedges.

Harvey: Some people in my younger days did call it a swaphook, but I always knew it as a faghook.

Ray: A word we still use today on the farm is *stopples*. They're the poach marks made in the fields by cows and horses.

Harvey: And here's another word you don't hear now, but that my grandparents always used. If they'd been out shopping and come back home the fire would be out. You see, we only had a downfire, what they call inglenooks now. You put a *cord* stick on. A cord's a piece of wood four feet long. It was a bit chilly like, and either grandmother or grandfather used to say, 'First thing, get that *yog* going.' I found out in later years that *yog* could be from Romany. It was used pretty frequently when I was a lad.'

Ray: I was brought up with lots of dialect words, but if I used them now you wouldn't know what I was talking about. I went to the doctor once, Mortuary Morgan in Horsham, a miserable old devil, and I said 'I've got a *powd*.' And he said, 'Powd? Powd?' He said, 'You got a bloody boil!'

Bob: Harvey's got one there, look, on the back of his neck.

Harvey: That's a blind powd. That means it never burst. That's been on there about 65 years. It's only through bad diet. My father used to have them. I had them when I was a lad.

Bob: People don't realize today what it's like to be hungry. It was hard in the countryside between the wars. When we were kids we always had worms. That's why we were all thin. I thought the reason kids today have got fat is that they don't have worms any more, but this woman told me the other day that they do. That surprised me.

Harvey: When I was kid, every Friday night, whether we wanted it or not, we had to have a cup of senna tea, which was made out of senna pods, a laxative. Every Friday night. It'd work by Sunday. And what made matters

worse, after dinner of a Sunday, we always had what mother called a sweet, which in season was stewed rhubarb with hardly any sugar. Well, you can imagine what that was like with the senna tea! And then, when the rhubarb season was finished, it would be stewed prunes, which had the same effect. I haven't eaten either since. Then you'd hurry away to the *dunnekin*.

Ray: Up the *dunnekin*, yes. That's what we called it, too.

Bob: It's where the Australians get their *dunny* from.

And at this point, suddenly remembering, Ray jumped up to find his copy of *Sussex Privies* for me to sign.

The accent and the memories are wonderful to hear, but I wondered whether I might still come across any of the old words still being used spontaneously, early in the 21st century. Enter Ron Saunders. Ron was born near Herstmonceux in 1921, worked all his life as a gardener and has the broadest Sussex accent you'll hear anywhere. Even more of a delight for me, however, was the verbal equivalent of an archaeologist turning the soil and uncovering a spread of ancient coins. Here he is recalling his school days:

'I was knocked down with 'oopin' cough. And when that got cleared up it left me with a weak 'eart. So when I first started school I could onie goo 'alf days: oosed to go in the mornin'. Then me mother oosed to come and fetch me 'ome dinnertime. I oosed to 'ave to lay up then till teatime. I never 'ad full schoolin'. That went roit on till I must have been six, seven year old.

'Later I went back full toim. The old 'eadmaster, he was a beggar, mate. 'E was so coarse wid yer, y'know, 'e never give you a chance. 'E used to bawl at yer. Do dis and do dat. Lots of toims it sort a frightened yer, bein' young.'

Ron Saunders

By *coarse*, Ron explains to me, he means rough-tongued rather than vulgar.

Now spot the ancient dialect word in this account of an incident during the Second World War. His gardening work was a reserved occupation, which meant that he was turned away by the recruiting officer. One associates white feathers with the First World War, but the idea clearly survived in this part of East Sussex.

'They oosed to run local dances, so I went up there one night. And they got all Canadians billeted round, all up in Ninfield village. So I went to this dance and went in an' was 'avin' a drink or so with some of the sodjers, see, and there was three or four girls – three I think it wus – I s'ppose they got thinkin'. They got in with these sodgers and what 'ave you, an' one of them come up to me, give me a matchbox, the old Swan Vestas match. When I opened it, was a white feather in it. And this sergeant I was talking to, cor! 'e went ver' near willocky. 'E went wild. 'E'd a gone down there and 'ed a bashed the bloody loif out of 'er! 'E didn't agree with it, but anyway 'is mates 'eld 'im off, quietened 'im down. I said, "Ah no, forget about it." I said, "You get oosed to that, bloody gels." I joined the 'Ome Guard in the end.'

To hear *willocky* was a heady triumph, but I was equally delighted with the climax of this account of Ron's gardening equipment.

'A lot of your tools you 'ad made by the ol' blacksmiths. All 'an'-made, the real

The blacksmith's forge in Chailey Green in the early 20th century

ol'-fashioned stuff. We 'ad what we called swaps, for cuttin' long grass, rubbish and that, but now they call them sickles. The same wid choppin' loitin' wood, we 'ad a 'an'bill. We called them 'an'bills, but a lot of people don't. 'Fertilizer? It was ornary farmyard then in my younger days, but roit now, the presen' moment, it's all artificial. Growmore and all that sort of stuff. What do they call the modern stuff? I can't think what it is – it's a *fantangled* name.'

Ron's last job was with the parks and gardens department at Bexhill.

'Damn good job. I retired at 62, an' I would 'ave carried on till 65, but the bloke that got the foreman's job I couldn't get on wid. 'E was all mouth and no do. What I mean by that is, 'e bin to college, got all the *sestificates*. When 'e come to the main job a seed sowin' and all loik, that e'd never done, so that was chucked on to me. And I said, "Well I en't 'avin that. Oim doin your work at sixty poun' a week". I said, "You get on wid it." So when the parks manager come round, I said "Roit, I want my papers. I want to pack up. I want to retire.' I said, "I can't get on with the bloke you brought in as foreman.'"

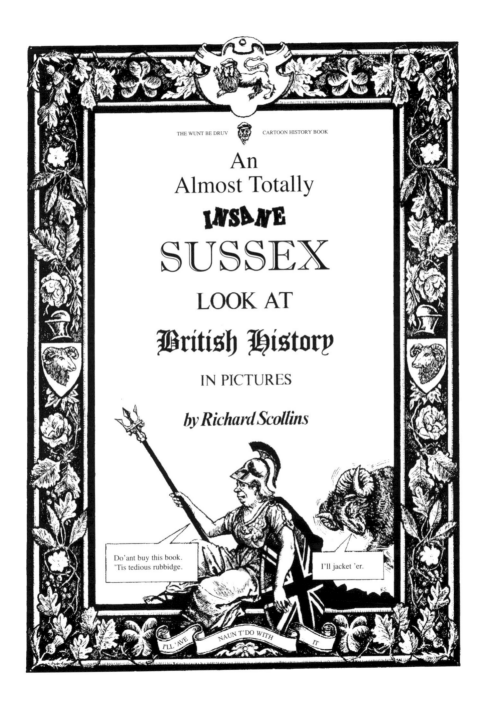

Alfred and the Cakes – AD 878

Canute Demonstrates His Inability to Turn the Tide – AD 1020

Lady Godiva – AD 1057

The Battle of Hastings – AD 1066

The Death of William Rufus - 1100

King John and Magna Carta – 1215

The Battle of Agincourt – 1415

Richard III at Bosworth - 1485

Henry VIII and Anne Boleyn – 1529

Raleigh and the Puddle – 1581

Francis Drake Goes Bowling – 1588

The Gunpowder Plot – 1605

The Execution of Charles I – 1649

Isaac Newton Discovers Gravity - 1666

**Bonnie Prince Charlie Arrives
in Scotland - 1745**

Nelson at Trafalgar – 1805

Wellington Inspects His Troops – 1815